Photos shot and developed
By
Brian Nguyen

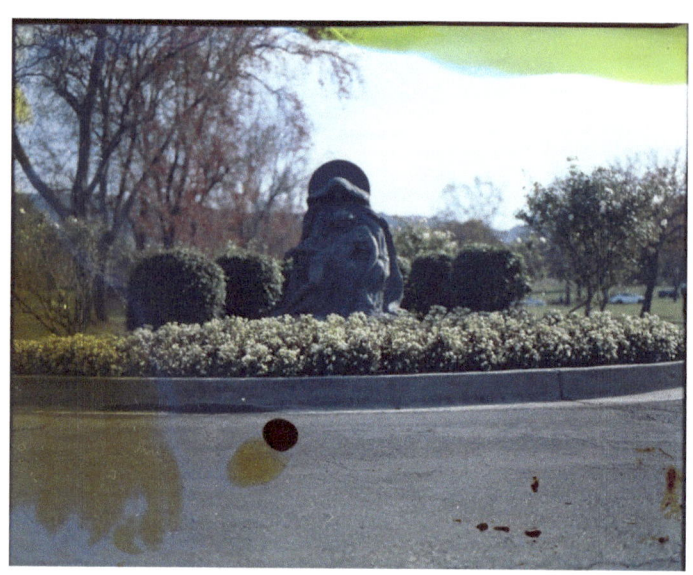

Cinestill 50d

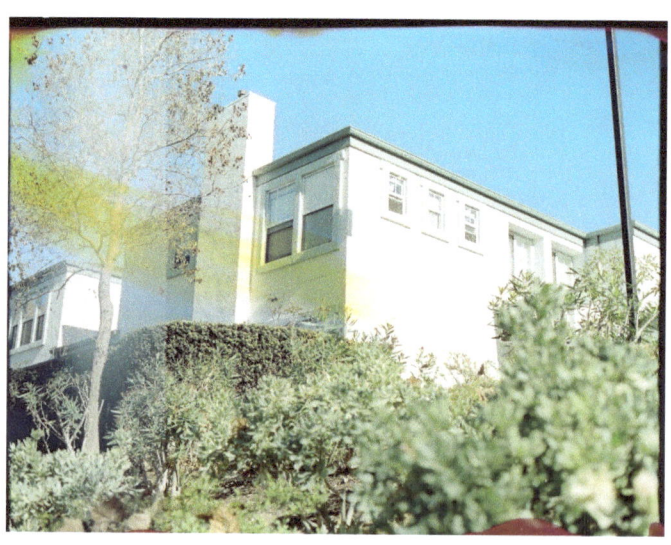

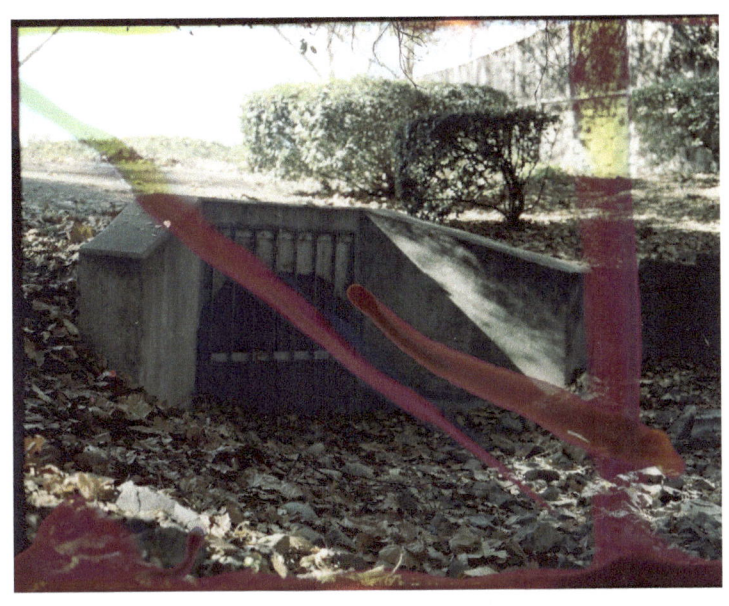

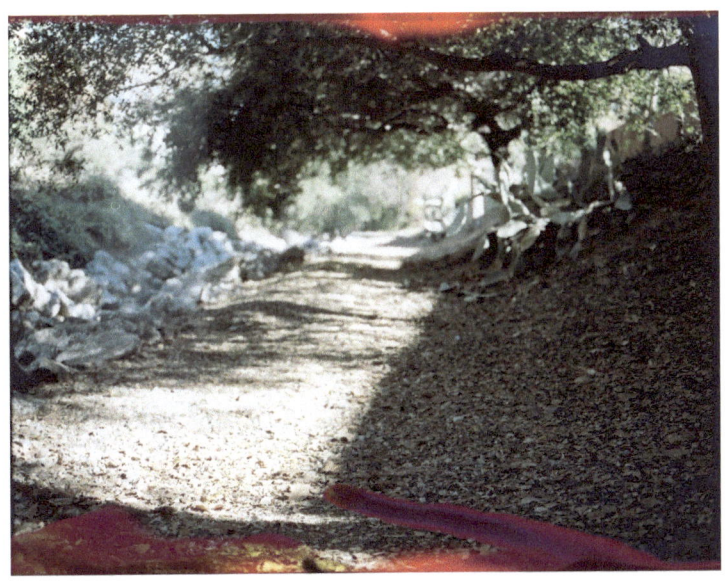

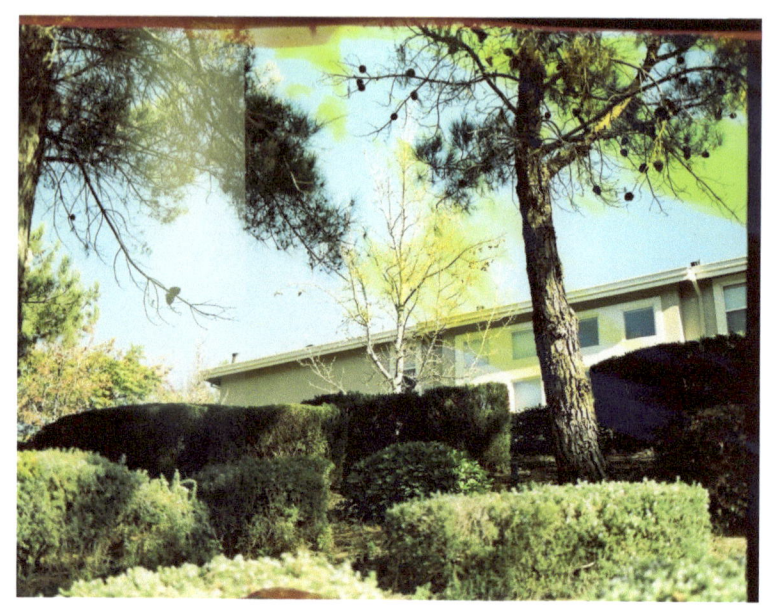

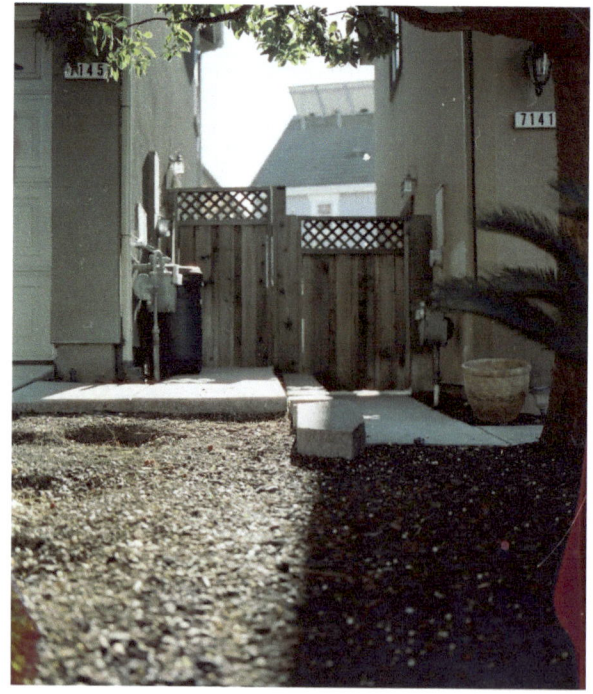

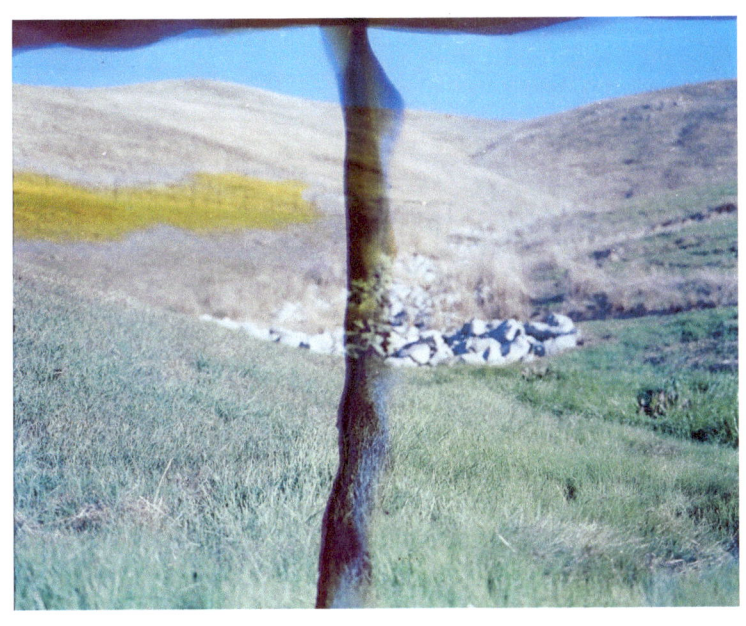

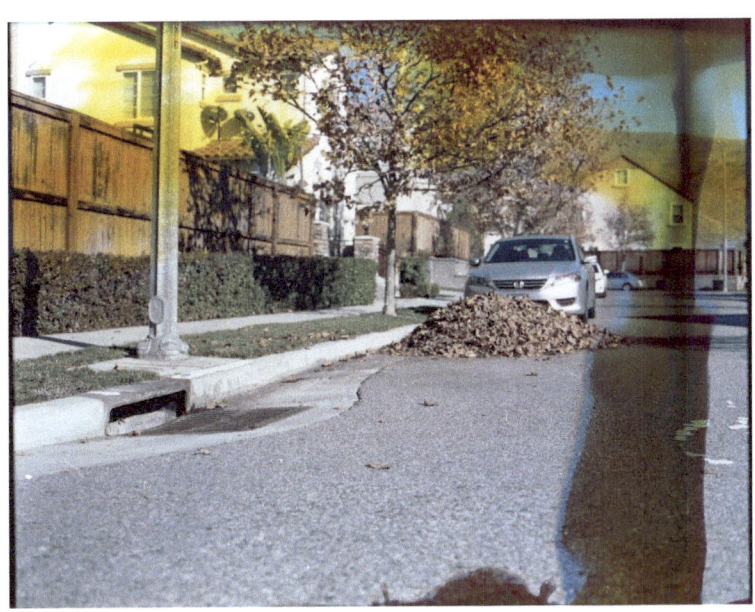

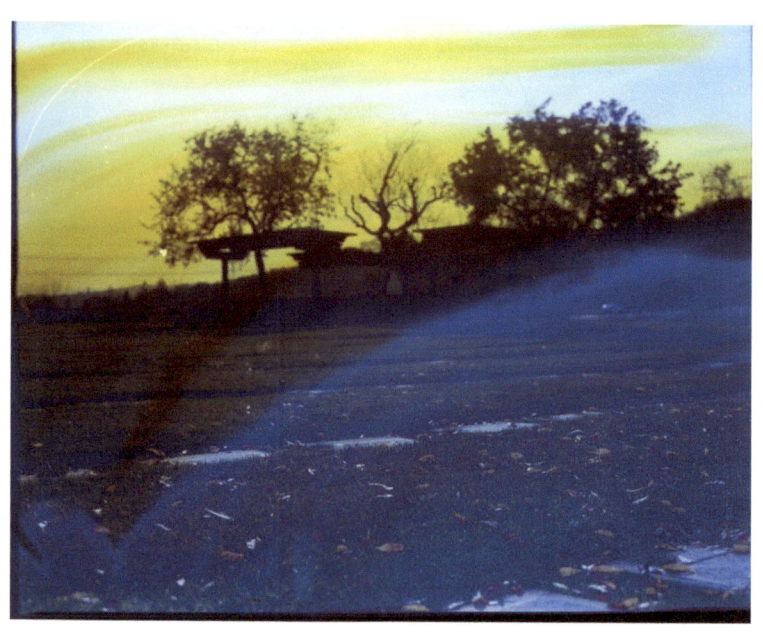

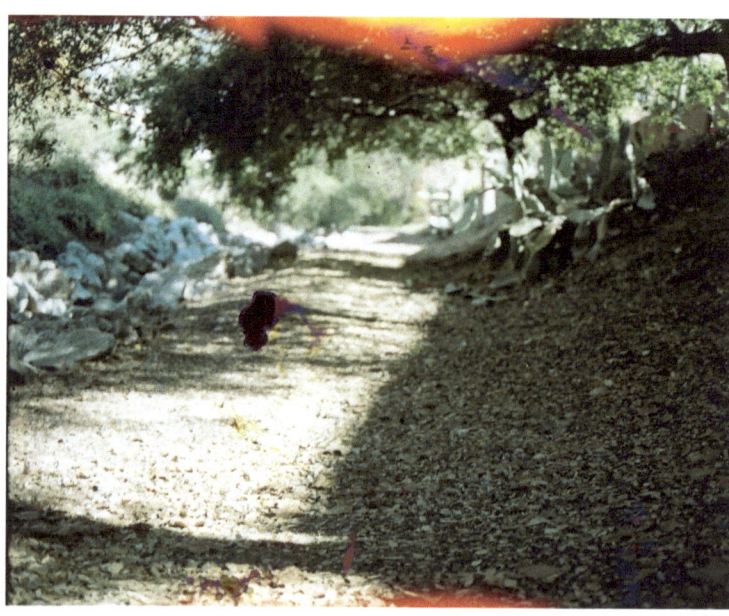

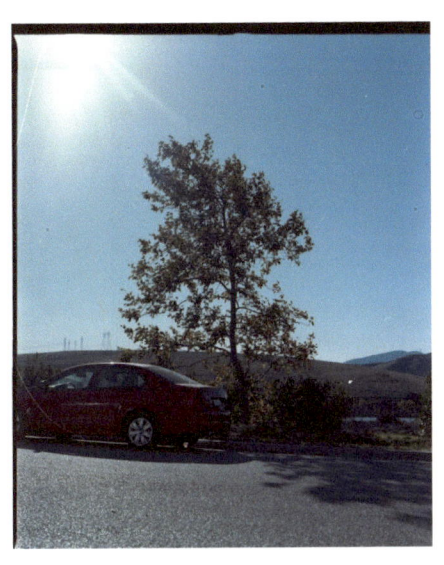
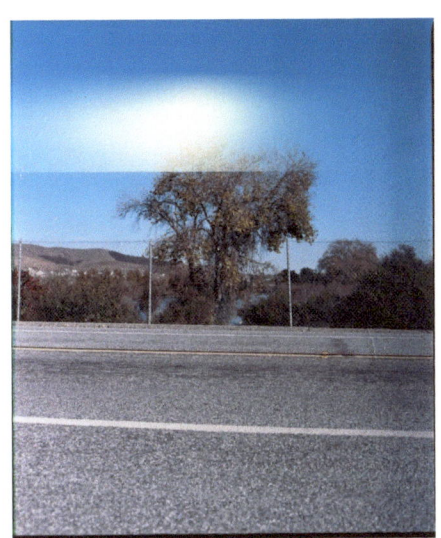

Ektar 100

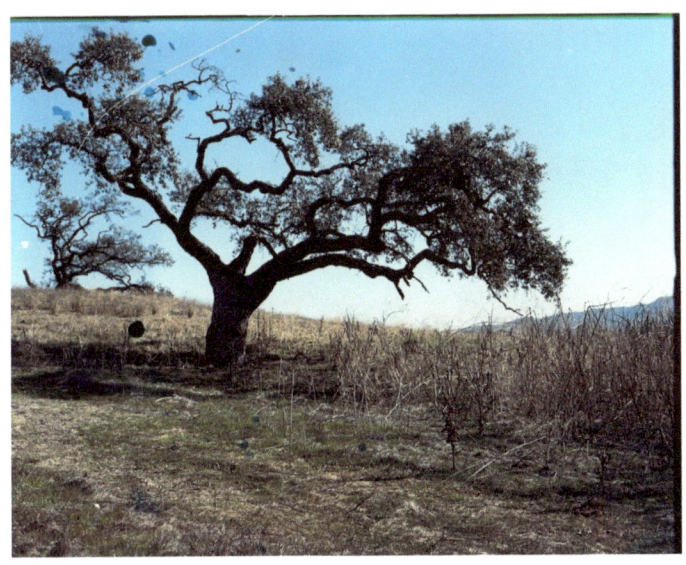

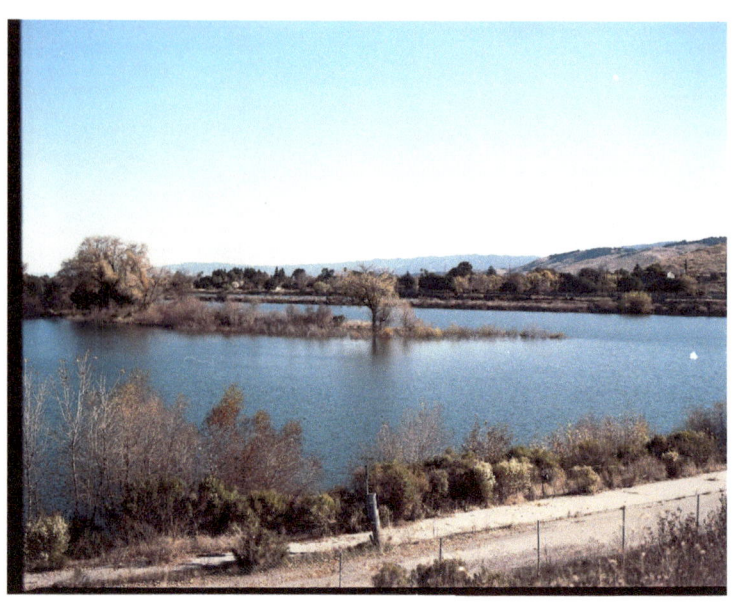

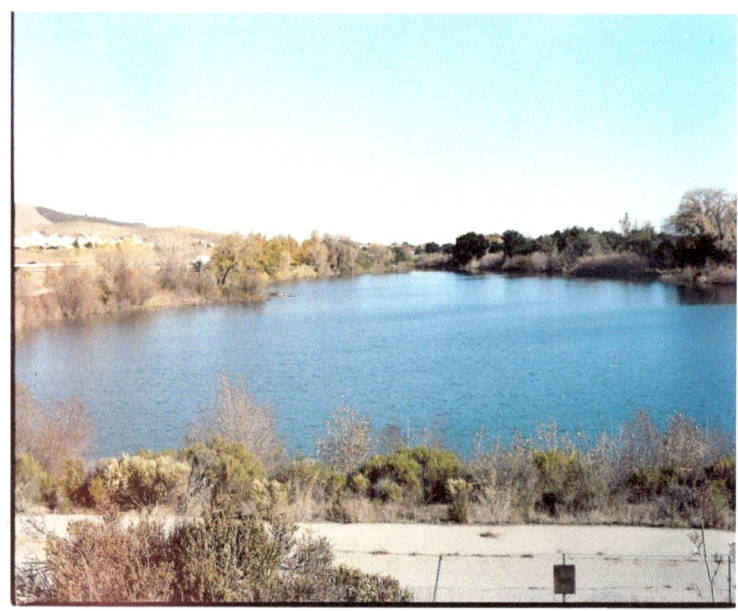

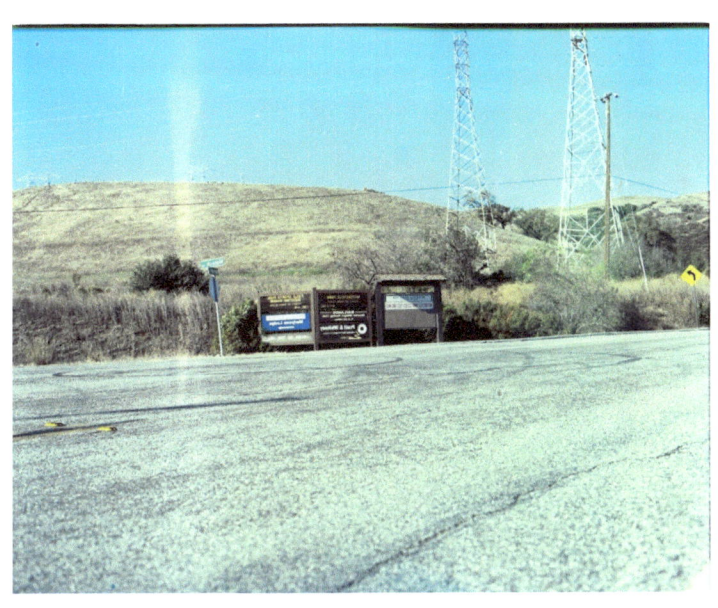

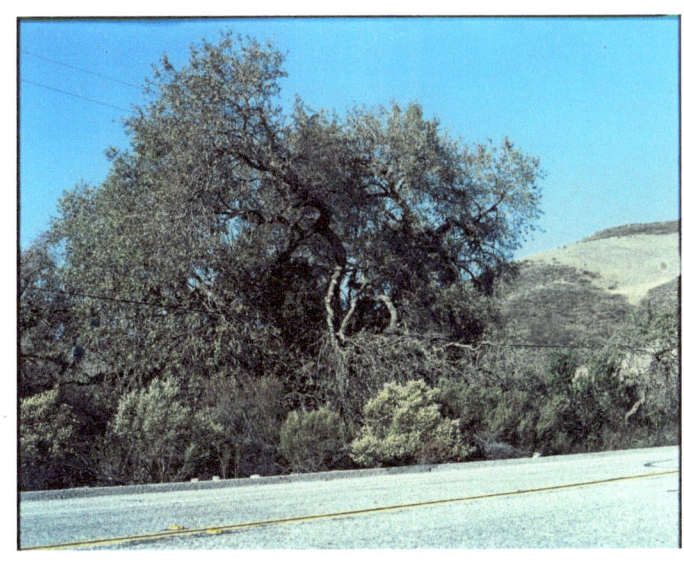

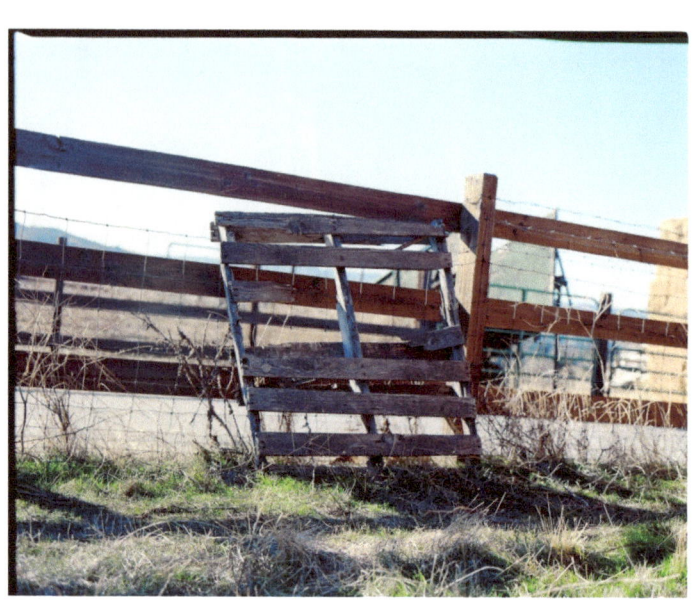

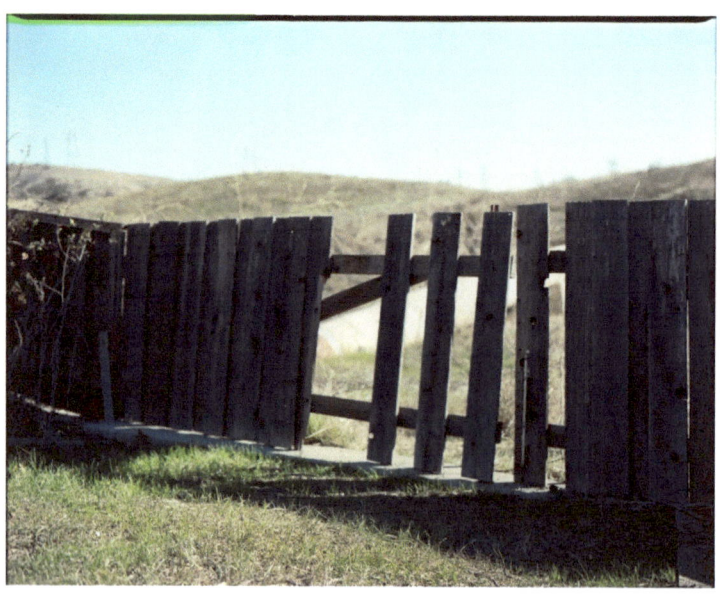

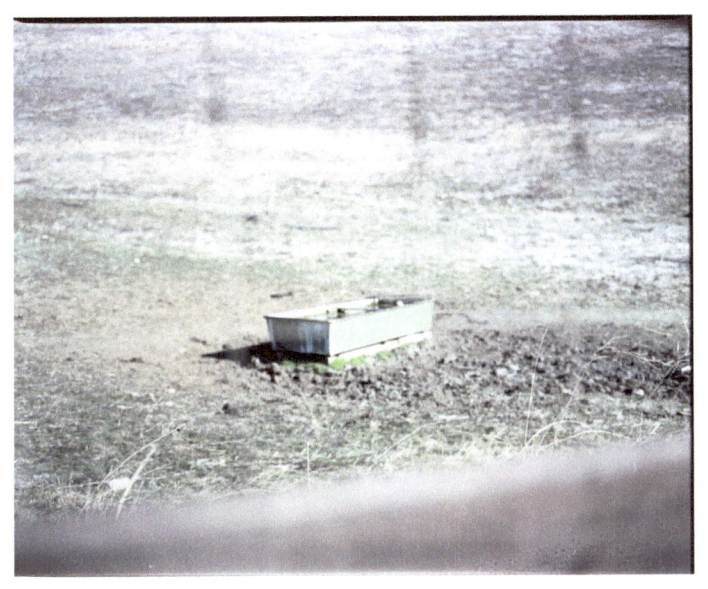

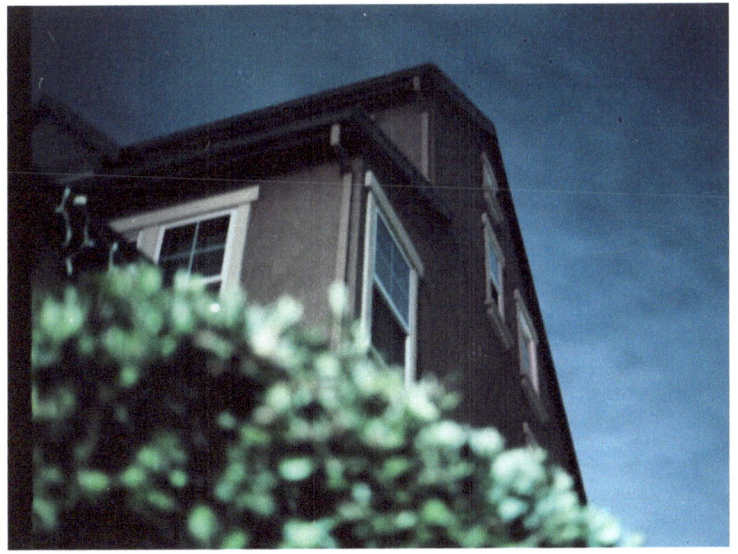

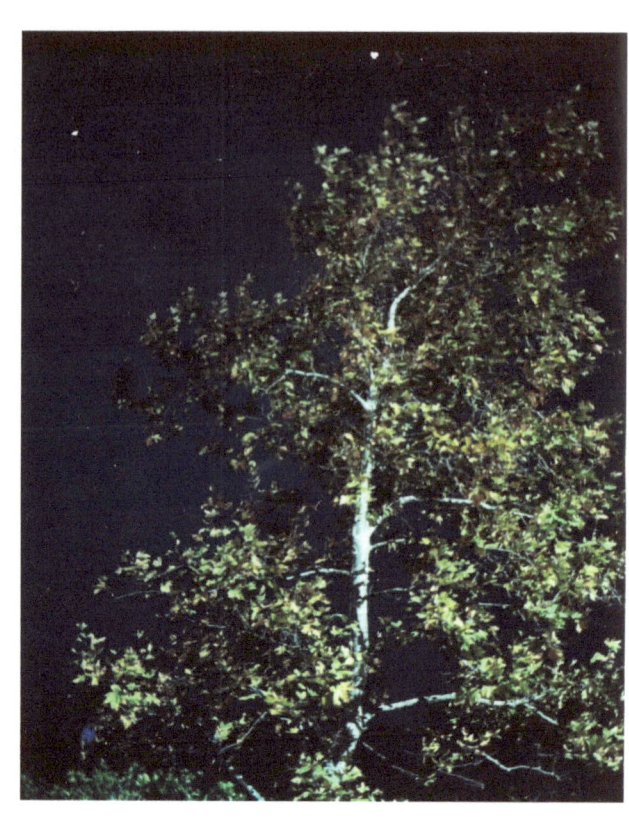

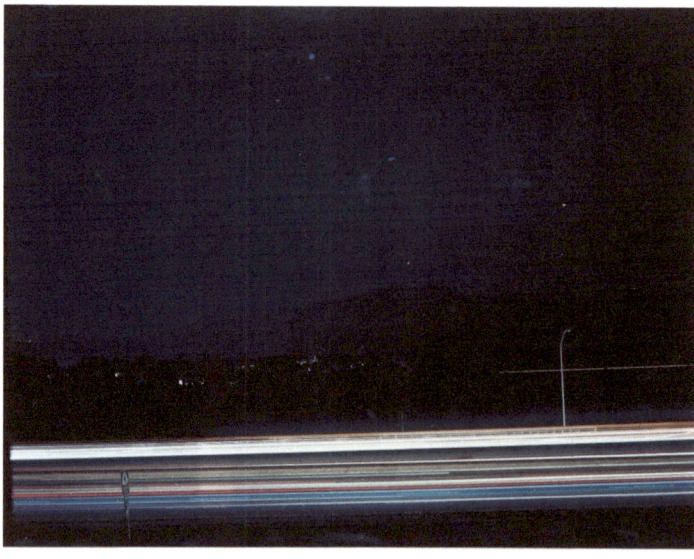

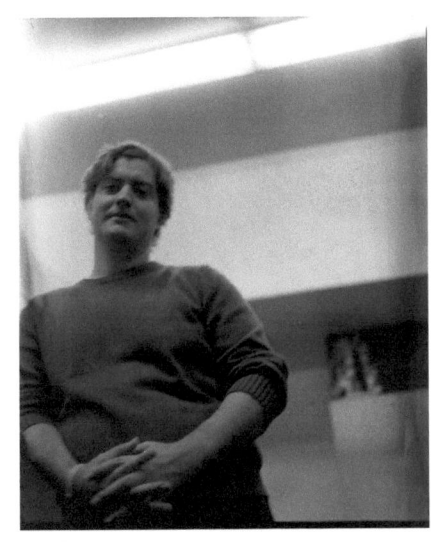
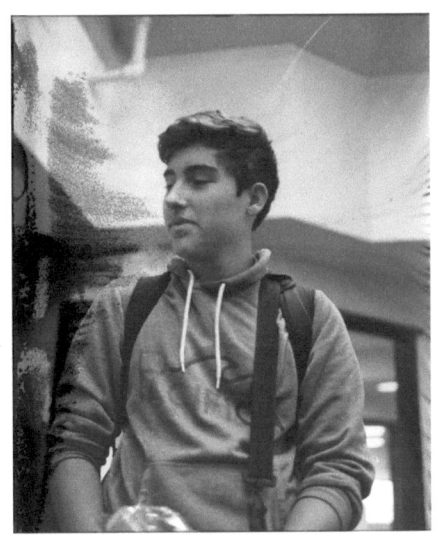

Tri-X 400

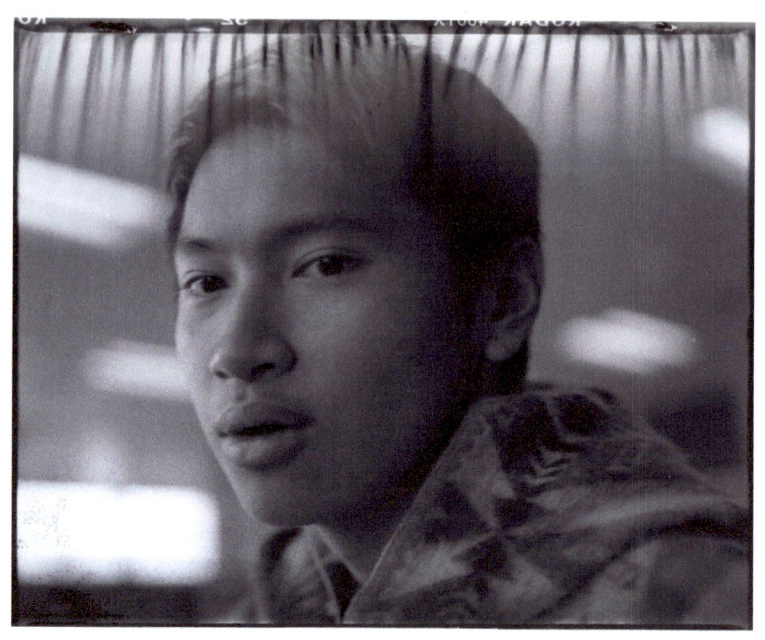

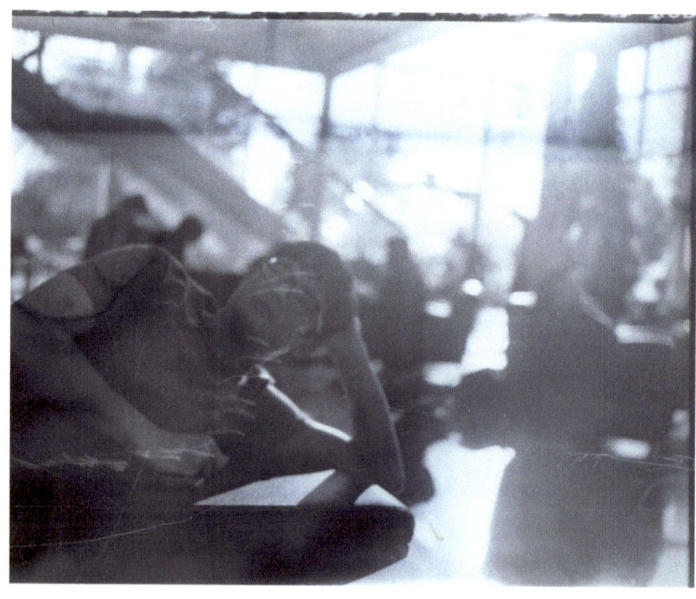

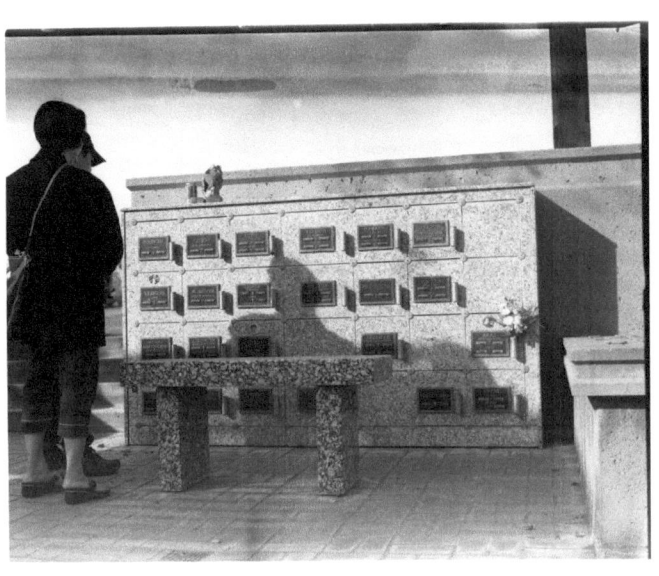

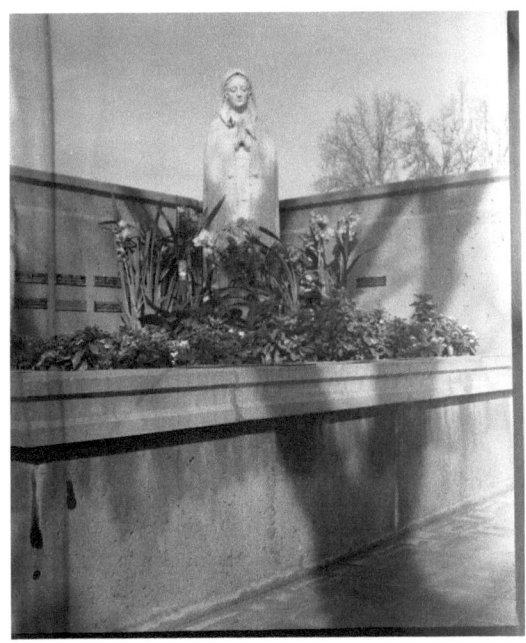

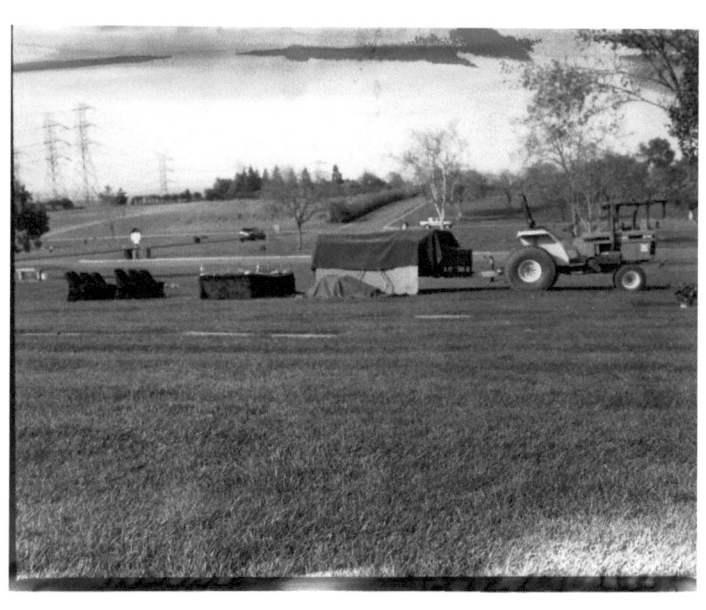

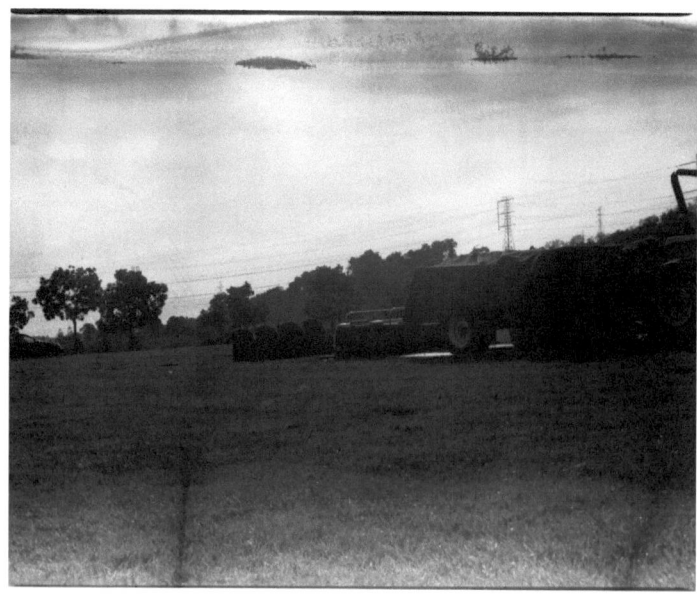

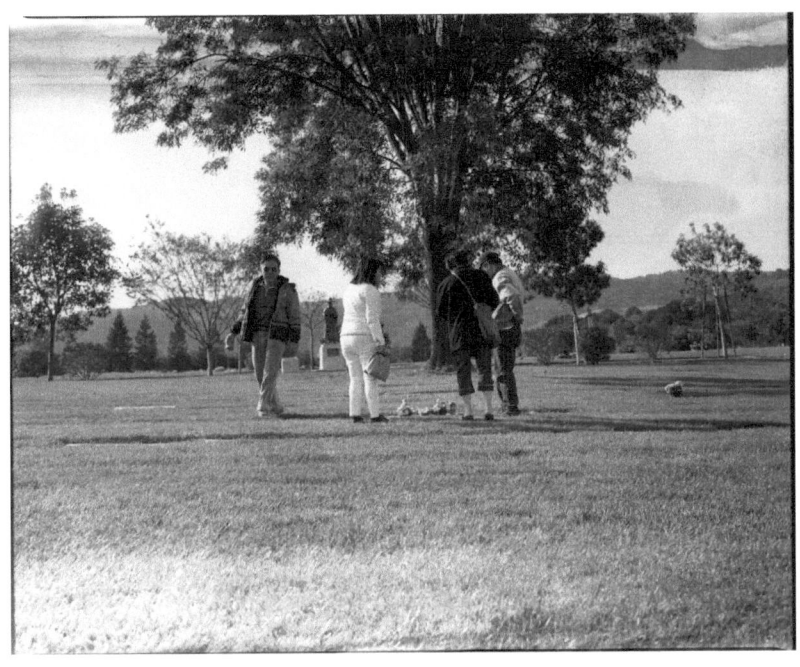

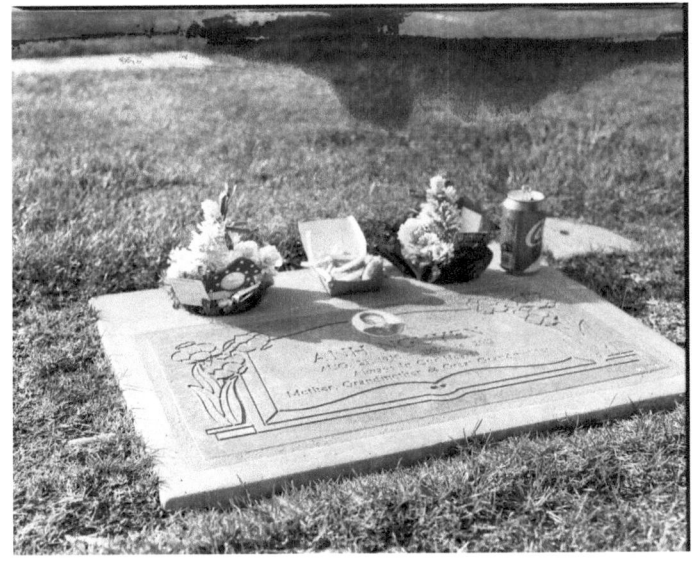

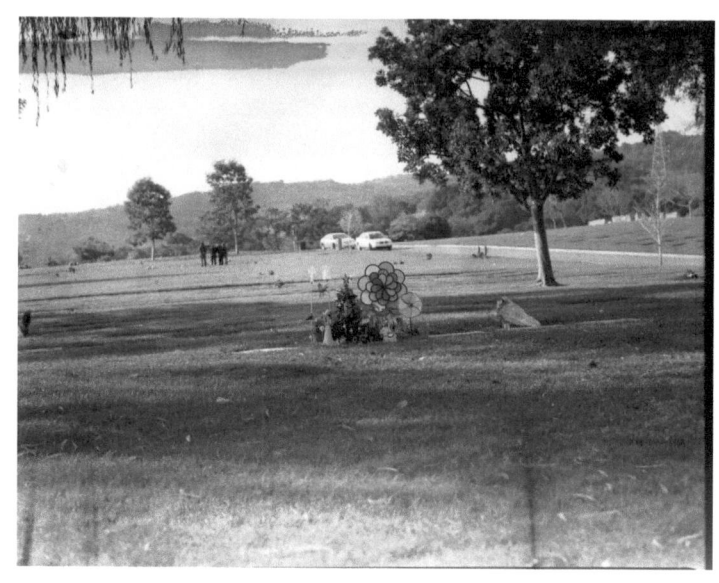

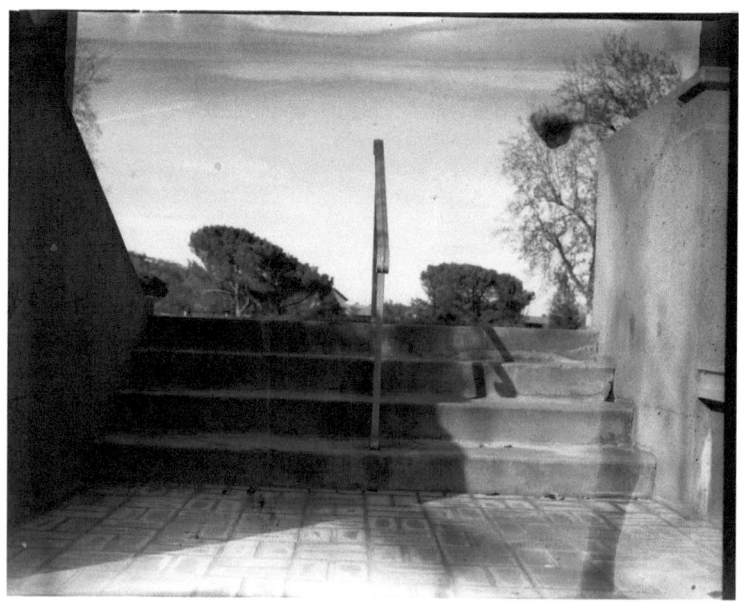

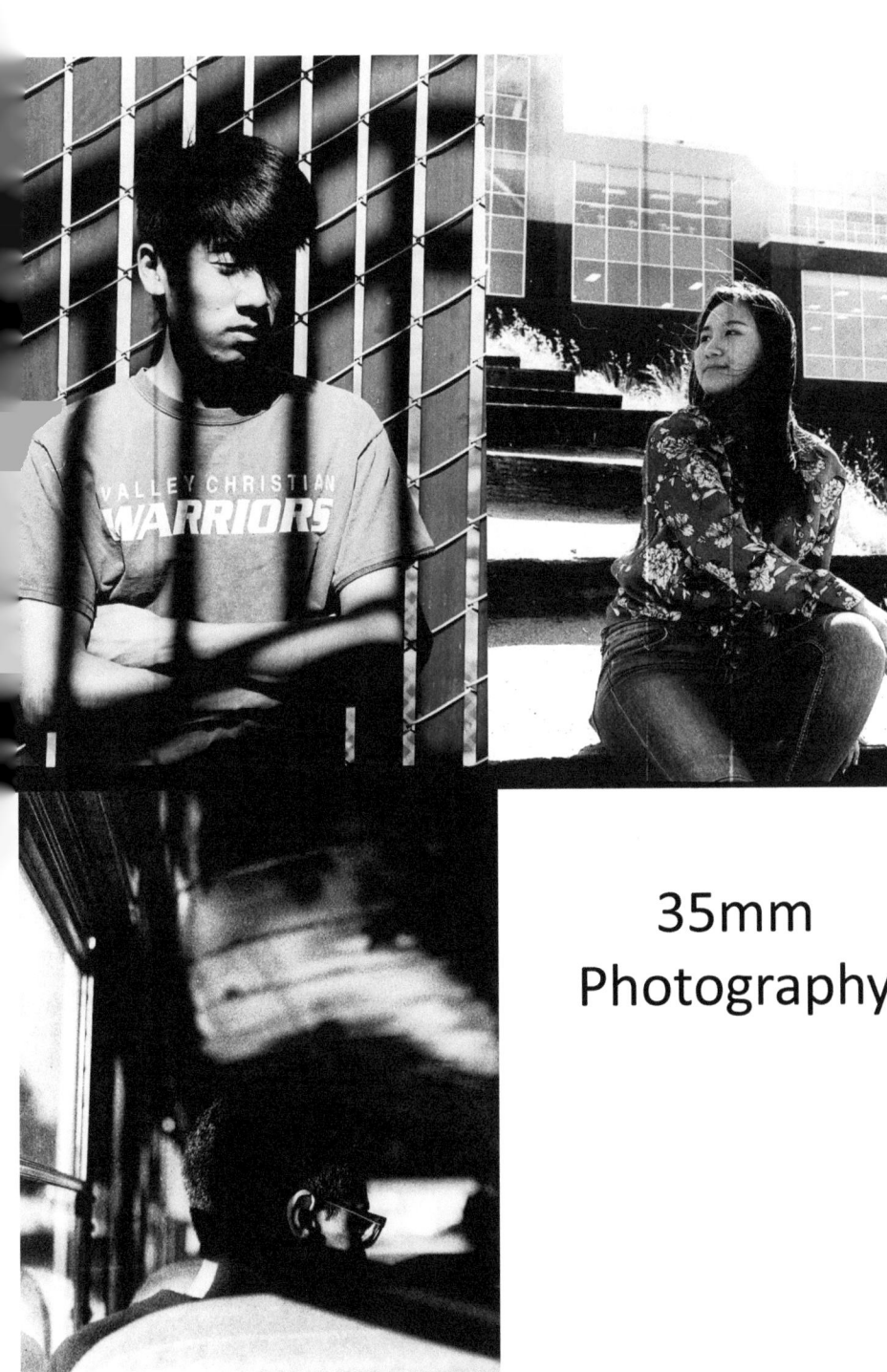

35mm Photography

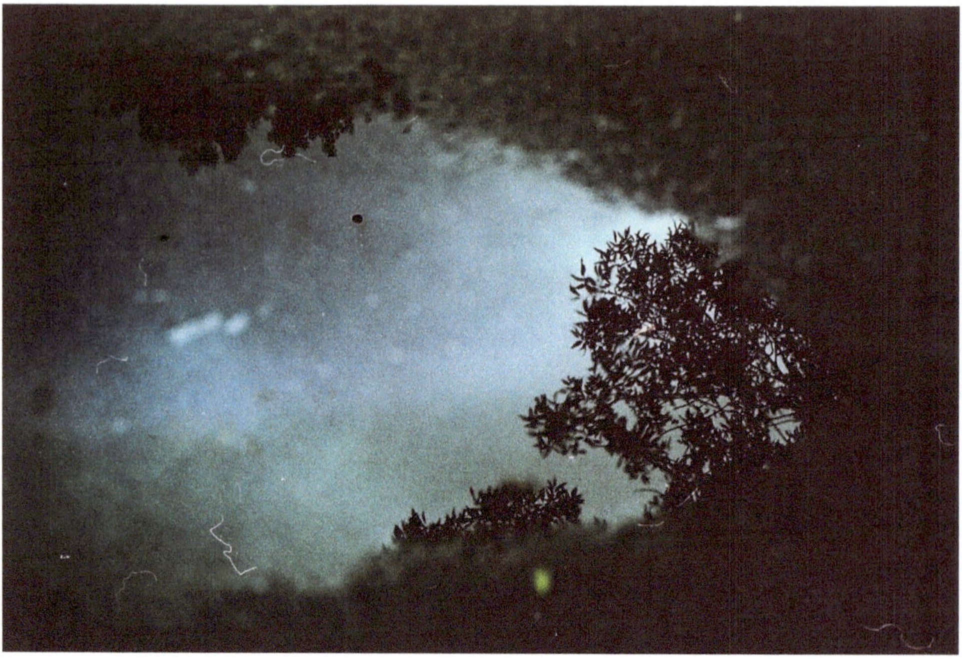

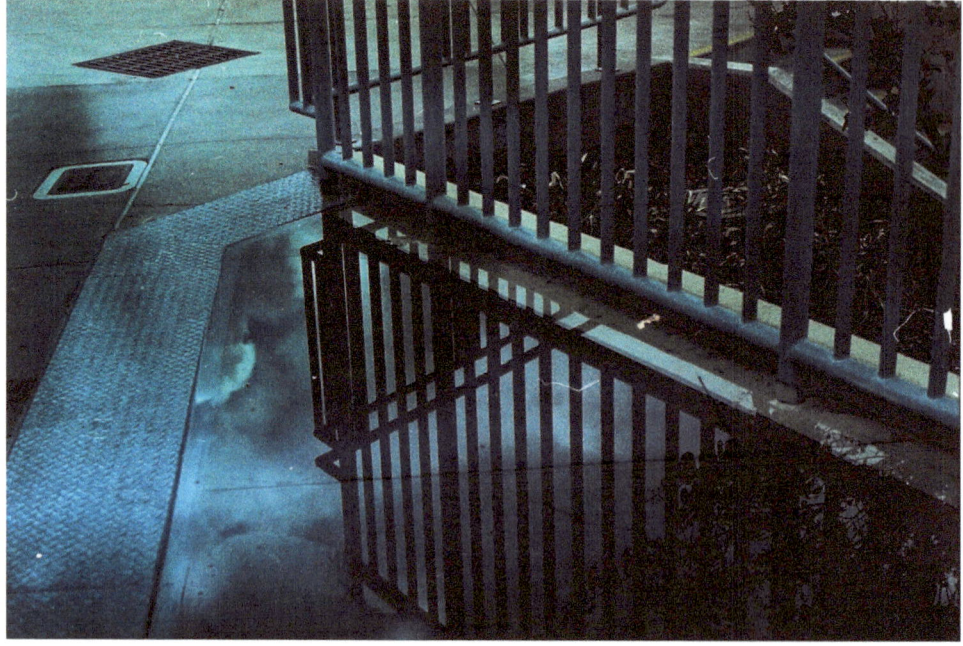

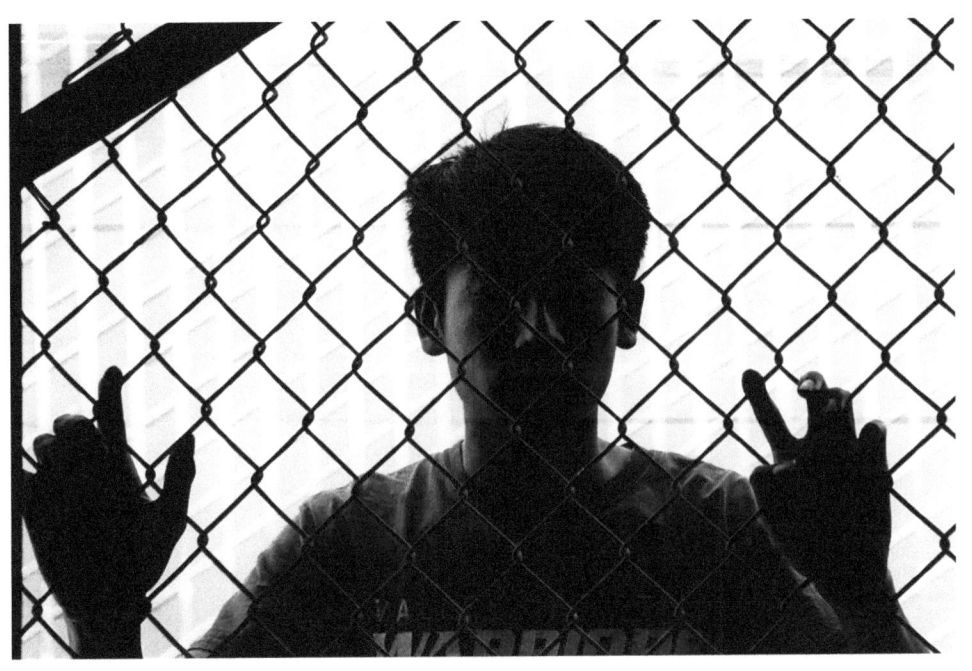

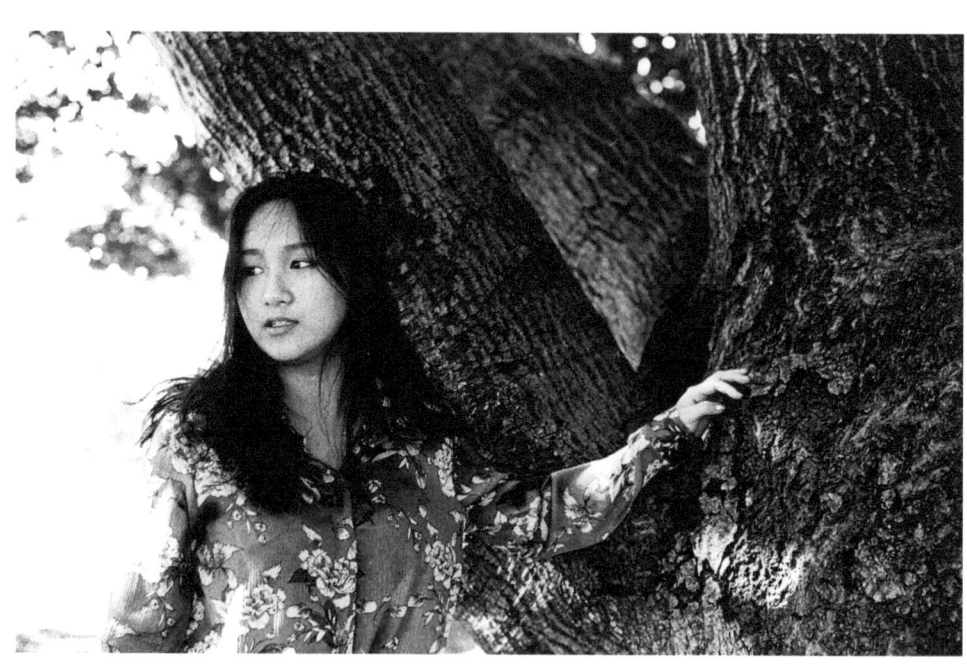

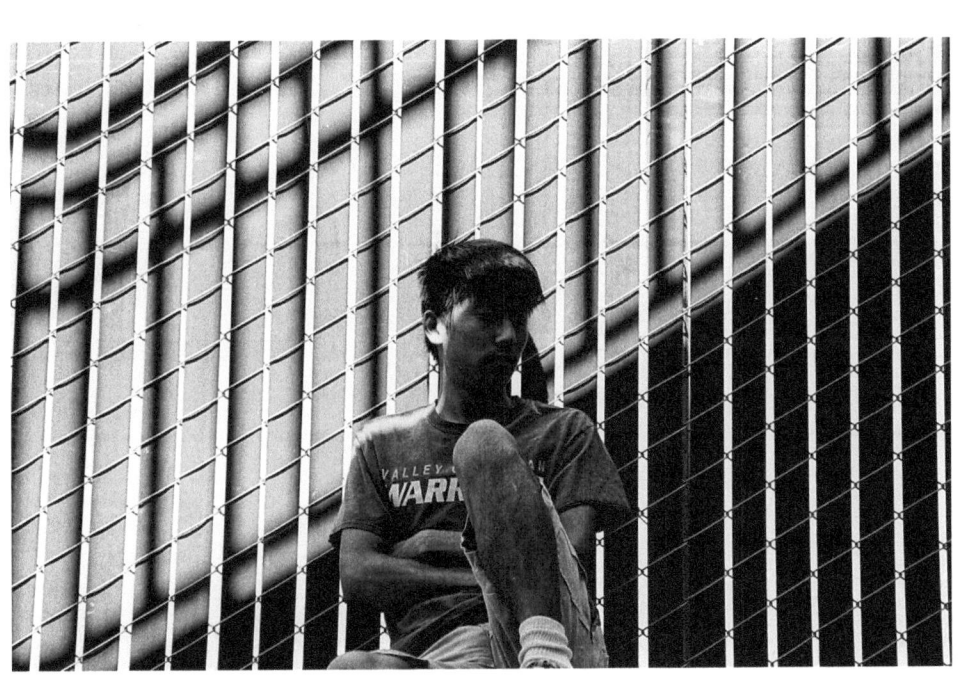

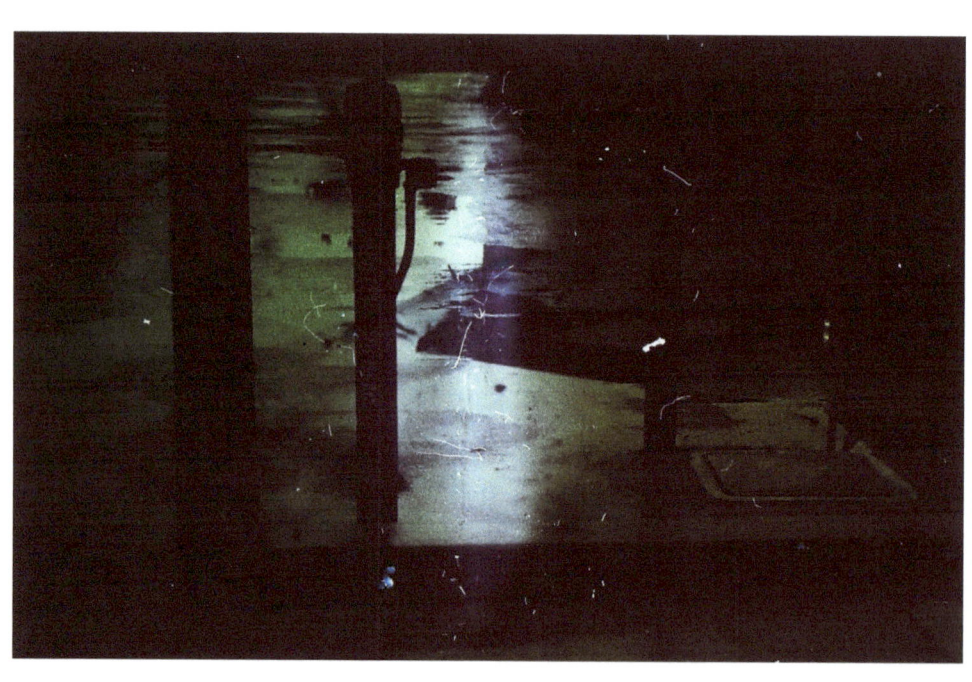

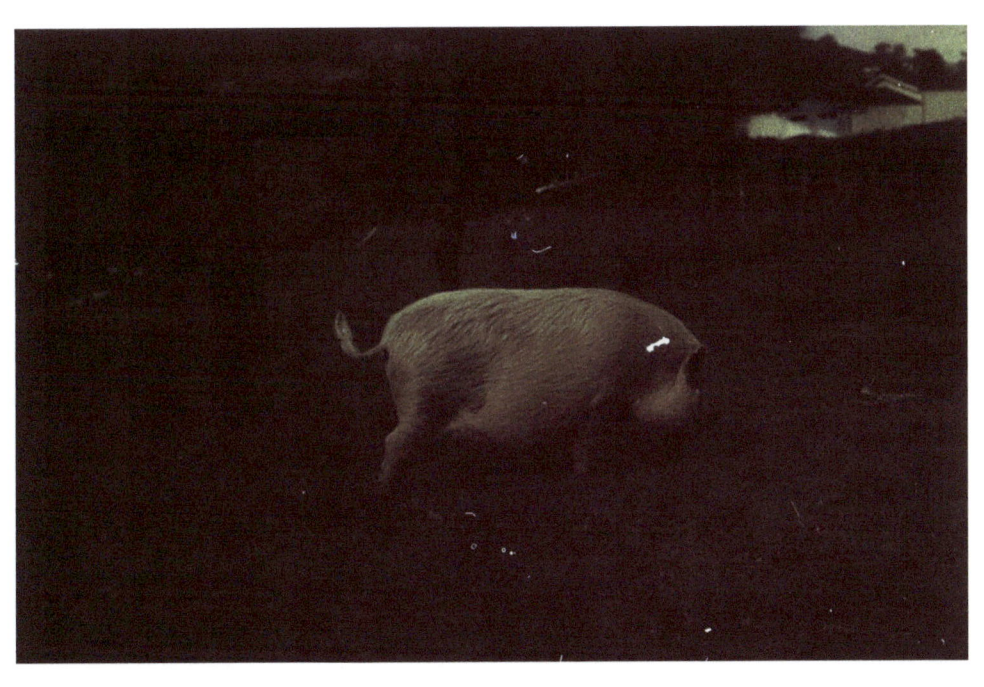

www.ingramcontent.com/pod-product-compliance
Lightning Source LLC
Chambersburg PA
CBHW040350220526
45473CB00009B/2844